Children Are No Match For Fire

A fire safety story for the whole family

Written by Carol Dean • **Illustrations by Sandra Dunn**

This educational project was sponsored by The National Association of State Fire Marshals

NASFM MISSION
…to protect human life, property
and the environment from fire.

The National Association of State Fire Marshals
offers its sincere thanks to Carol Dean, the author,
Sandra Dunn, the illustrator, and to all the professionals
that contributed their time to reviewing the manuscript.

The Association, the author and the illustrator express
their thanks to the Department of Justice's Office of
Juvenile Justice and Delinquency Prevention for the
partial funding that made this project possible.
(Grant #1999-JS-FX-0005).

For book orders go to: www.firemarshals.org

Published by: NASFM
National Association of State Fire Marshals
1319 F Street, N.W., Suite 301
Washington, D.C. 20004

Printed in China By Oceanic Graphic Printing (USA), Inc.
Hackensack, NJ 07601

Cover and interior design by Lindy Gifford

ISBN 0-615-12979-X

Library of Congress

It was July third at the fire station. Fire Chief Foley and his dalmatian Patches were teaching a group of children about fire safety and prevention.

STOP

DROP

ROLL

CRAWL LOW UNDER SMOKE

Patches was a trained fire dog. He loved showing the boys and girls how to *Stop, Drop, and Roll,* and to *crawl low under smoke.* He was even trained to sniff out dangerous things like matches, lighters, and fireworks.

The twins, John and Jodie, listened to Chief Foley, and watched Patches carefully. After practicing the fire safety drills, they received a certificate with their name on it. Before leaving the station, the twins shared the news that they had a birthday tomorrow.

Chief Foley smiled and wished them a happy and safe celebration. "Don't forget to practice the safety drills at home," he said.

John and Jodie promised to tell their parents about all they had learned, and waved good-bye to the chief and Patches as they hurried to meet their mother.

July Fourth finally arrived. Everyone was busy. Jodie watched as Mom worked in the kitchen frosting the cake.

"Can you put the candles in a heart shape on the cake?" Jodie asked.

Her mother smiled and nodded. She counted out 10 candles, five for each child. Jodie watched as her mother placed them carefully in the center of the cake.

"Do we have matches to light the candles?" Jodie inquired.

"Yes, of course. They are in a safe place until we need them," said her mother. "You know matches are tools, not toys, right?"

"Yes, Mommy. When we visited Chief Foley and Patches at the fire station, they taught us many lessons about fire prevention and fireworks. Our job is to discuss and practice fire safety this weekend with our family.

Jodie looked at the notes she received at the fire station. "We have to:
- Not touch matches and lighters, and tell adults if we see them.
- Not play with fireworks, not even sparklers.
- Stop, Drop, and Roll if our clothes catch on fire.
- Crawl low under smoke and practice fire-exit drills at home."

"You learned all that from Chief Foley and Patches. That's wonderful! We'll get the whole family involved this weekend."

In the backyard, Dad was getting the grill ready. He used a lighter to get the charcoal going. Poof! The flames leaped up. Dad quickly put the lighter away out of sight. He knew it was his job to keep such things out of a young child's reach. Lighters were adult tools, not toys.

John ran outside to watch his father. John was drawn to fire. He started jumping up and down. "John, what are you doing?" Dad asked.

"I'm dancing like the fire," John answered.

"John, that is very creative, and good exercise, but let's not forget that fire can hurt you. You need to stay at least three feet away from the grill. Do you remember that rule?"

"Yes, Dad, I remember." John continued his dance at a safe distance. It was his birthday and he wanted to celebrate.

"How was your fire safety class with Chief Foley and Patches?" Dad inquired.

John stopped jumping for a minute, excited to tell his father all about the visit to the fire station. "It was great Dad. Chief Foley taught us that sparklers are not toys and dangerous for children. Those little sparkling sticks get *really* hot, like up to 2000 degrees!

"That could burn your skin and set your clothes on fire. And if you step or fall on them it could hurt a lot and you might have to go to the hospital."

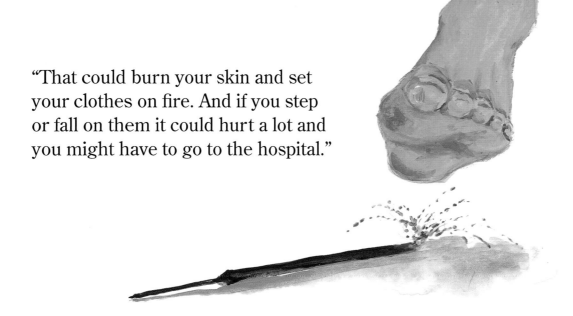

"If fire gets on your clothes you have to stop, drop, and roll. Patches showed us how to do that."

STOP　　　**DROP**　　　**ROLL**

"If there is a fire in our house, we need to practice how to escape from our bedrooms, crawl low, and go quick to our meeting place."

CRAWL LOW UNDER SMOKE

"I'm proud of you John for remembering so much. We'll get the family to practice later," Dad said as he took the burgers off the grill.

Aunt Barbara and Aunt Nancy arrived with their children and more food.

HAPPY BIRTHDAY TO YOU

After the meal, Mom appeared carrying the birthday cake. Everyone sang the Happy Birthday song to John and Jodie. Mom lit the candles and John and Jodie leaned forward to blow them out. Jodie got too close. The pretty ribbon on her shirt almost touched the flame.

"Jodie, look out!" Mother yelled. Jodie pulled back just in time. "Okay Jodie, you said you were going to practice fire safety this weekend. Show me how you would Stop, Drop, and Roll if that shirt had caught on fire."

Jodie proudly demonstrated. She dropped to the ground, covered her
face with her hands, and rolled back and forth just as Chief Foley and
Patches had taught her. Everyone clapped and cheered! "Good job!"

"Your turn, John," Dad shouted. "Let's see what you would do if a sparkler caught your clothes on fire."

John sprang into action rolling back and forth. Again everyone cheered and clapped. John got Dave, Mike, and Tammy to practice, too.

The family cleared the table and headed for the lake to see the fireworks. It was very crowded, and there were sparklers glowing everywhere.

John looked around for his friends. He saw his neighbor Kim. Kim turned and backed up to wave to John. She didn't see the boy waving a sparkler behind her. Within seconds her dress was on fire. She screamed!

Not good, John thought. He remembered what Chief Foley had said. "Kim, Stop! Drop! Roll!" he shouted as he ran toward her. The frightened girl did what John said.

Kim's mother came running when she heard the cries. Her daughter was rolling back and forth with help from John. Finally the fire on her dress was out. Her mom scooped up Kim, and squeezed her tight. She was safe thanks to John.

Chief Foley was at the celebration and came running. "Wow, that was a close one, John. I need to thank you for paying attention in fire safety class. You just saved that young lady from severe burns and a trip to the hospital. It would not have been a good Fourth of July for her."

Chief Foley paused, "Please excuse me for a minute John,
I need to go talk to that young man and his parents.
They need a safety lesson on the dangers of sparklers."

John felt good. It was a birthday he would never forget. The TV cameras were there to interview him, and said he was a hero. Chief Foley presented John with a honorary Junior Fire Marshal award for his quick action in helping to save Kim.

When John was asked what he thought of the whole thing, he replied, "I think I want to be a firefighter when I grow up, and I'm going to teach children that they are no match for fire."

Safety things to talk about!

Tell an adult when you find matches or a lighter. Are matches and lighters in a safe place?

Make sure candles are out when you leave the room. Even Birthday candles can be dangerous!

Do you know how to Stop, Drop, and Roll? Show your family what you have learned. Do it now!

STOP   **DROP**   **ROLL**

Fireworks are dangerous. Even sparklers can hurt you! Let the professionals handle them.

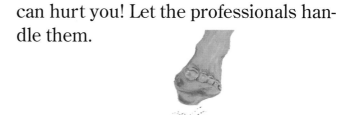

Practice exit drills in your home often! Are your smoke detectors working? Don't forget to crawl low and go, go, go, to your meeting place outside!

CRAWL LOW UNDER SMOKE

Look for EXIT signs everywhere you go (hint: in places like movie theaters, stores, hotels, and restaurants). In an emergency, remember to take the stairs, not the elevator! You don't have much time, and there may be more than one way out!

You can be a Honorary Junior Fire Marshal, too!
Practice fire safety with your family! Then photocopy the form on the next page. Fill in your name and share your safety skills with others. Check out some fun web sites on the last page!

FIRE SAFETY CERTIFICATE

Presented to

_____

by

_____

for practicing fire safety and prevention with family.

Honorary Junior Fire Marshal

Games and Fun Web Sites

★ **Burn Institute:** http://www.burninstitute.org/ Be a Fire-safe kid. Take the online challenge and test your knowledge. Then print out the certificate with your name on it.

★ **Canada's Staying Alive:** http://www.stayingalive.ca
Help Fire Lobster escape from the fire. Listen to Mrs. About Fire and Flip to help guide you through the Great Escape!

★ **CPSC Kids Site:** http://www.cpsc.gov/kids/kidsafety/
Click on Kidd's bike for an exciting ride to the park.

★ **Fireproof Children:** http://www.playsafebesafe.com
Have fun with the keep away card game for 3 year olds and up.

★ **Risk Watch® Program Kids Page:**
http://www.nfpa.org/riskwatch/kids.html#
Games for readers and non-readers.

★ **Smokey Bear's Kids Page:**
http://www.smokeybear.com/kids/default.asp
Help your Smoke Jumpers extinguish the fires.

★ **Sparky® the Fire Dog:**
http://www.nfpa.org/sparky/
Lots of great games about fire safety.

★ **USFA Kids Page:**
http://www.usfa.fema.gov/kids/html/index.shtm
Can you find all of the hazards in Hydro's Hazard House?

If you would like to learn more about the National Association of State Fire Marshals, go to www.firemarshals.org.